oriental

COMPLETE COOKERY

This is a Starfire book
First published in 2001

04 05 03

5 7 9 10 8 6 4

Starfire is part of
The Foundry Creative Media Company Limited
Crabtree Hall, Crabtree Lane, Fulham, London, SW6 6TY

Visit the Foundry website: www.foundry.co.uk/recipes

ISBN: 1-903817-10-2

The CIP record for this book is available from the British Library.

Printed in Poland

ACKNOWLEDGEMENTS

Authors: Catherine Atkinson, Juliet Barker, Liz Martin, Gina
Steer, Carol Tennant, Mari Mererid Williams and Elizabeth Wolf-Cohen
Photography: Colin Bowling, Paul Forrester and Stephen Brayne
Home Economists and Stylists: Jacqueline Bellefontaine,
Mandy Phipps, Vicki Smallwood and Penny Stephens

All props supplied by Barbara Stewart at Surfaces

NOTE
Recipes using uncooked eggs should be avoided by infants,
the elderly, pregnant women and anyone suffering from an illness.

MEAT

FISH & SHELLFISH

CONTENTS

SOUPS & STARTERS

oriental

COMPLETE COOKERY

POULTRY

RICE & NOODLES

VEGETABLES

ENTERTAINING

Hygiene in the Kitchen

I t is well worth remembering that many foods can carry some form of bacteria. In most cases, the worst it will lead to is a bout of food poisoning or gastroenteritis, although for certain groups this can be more serious – the risk can be reduced or eliminated by good food hygiene and proper cooking.

Do not buy food that is past its sell-by date and do not consume any food that is past its use-by date. When buying food, use the eyes and nose. If the food looks tired, limp or a bad colour or it has a rank, acrid or simply bad smell, do not buy or eat it under any circumstances.

Do take special care when preparing raw meat and fish. A separate chopping board should be used for each; wash the knife, board and the hands thoroughly before handling or preparing any other food.

Regularly clean, defrost and clear out the refrigerator or freezer – it is worth checking the packaging to see exactly how long each product is safe to freeze.

Avoid handling food if suffering from an upset stomach as bacteria can be passed through food preparation.

Dish cloths and tea towels must be washed and changed regularly. Ideally use disposable cloths, which should be replaced on a daily basis. More durable cloths should be left to soak in bleach, then washed in the washing machine on a boil wash.

Keep the hands, cooking utensils and food preparation surfaces clean and do not allow pets to climb on to any work surfaces.

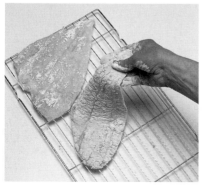

BUYING

A void bulk buying where possible, especially fresh produce such as meat, poultry, fish, fruit and vegetables unless buying for the freezer. Fresh foods lose their nutritional value rapidly so buying a little at a time minimises loss of nutrients. It also eliminates a packed refrigerator, which reduces the effectiveness of the refrigeration process.

When buying prepackaged goods such as cans or pots of cream and yogurts, check that the packaging is intact and not damaged or pierced at all. Cans should not be dented, pierced or rusty. Check the sell-by dates even for cans and packets of dry ingredients such as flour and rice. Store fresh foods in the refrigerator as soon as possible – not in the car or the office.

When buying frozen foods, ensure that they are not heavily iced on the outside and the contents feel completely frozen. Ensure that the frozen foods have been stored in the cabinet at the correct

storage level and the temperature is below -18°C/ -4°F. Pack in cool bags to transport home and place in the freezer as soon as possible after purchase.

PREPARATION

M ake sure that all work surfaces and utensils are clean and dry. Hygiene should be given priority at all times.

Separate chopping boards should be used for raw and cooked meats, fish and vegetables. Currently, a variety of good-quality plastic boards come in various designs and colours. This makes differentiating easier and the plastic has the added hygienic advantage of being washable at high temperatures in the dishwasher. (NB: If using the board for fish, first wash in cold water, then in hot to prevent odour!) Also, remember that knives and utensils should always be cleaned thoroughly after use.

When cooking, be particularly careful to keep cooked and raw food separate to avoid any con-tamination. It is worth washing all fruits and vegetables regardless of whether they are going to be eaten raw or lightly cooked. This rule should apply even to prewashed herbs and salads.

Do not reheat food more than once. If using a microwave, always check that the food is piping hot all the way through. (In theory, the food should reach 70°C/158°F and needs to be cooked at that temperature for at least three minutes to ensure that all bacteria are killed.)

All poultry must be thawed thoroughly before using, including chicken and poussin. Remove the food to be thawed from the freezer and place in a shallow dish to contain the juices. Leave the food in the refrigerator until it is thawed completely. A 1.4 kg/3 lb whole chicken will take about 26–30 hours to thaw. To speed up the process immerse the chicken in cold water. However, make sure that the water is changed regularly. When the joints can move freely and no ice crystals remain in the cavity, the bird is thawed completely.

Once thawed, remove the wrapper and pat the chicken dry. Place the chicken in a shallow dish, cover lightly and store as close to the base of the refrigerator as possible. The chicken should be cooked as soon as possible.

Some foods can be cooked from frozen including many prepacked foods such as soups, sauces, casseroles and breads. Where applicable follow the manufacturers' instructions.

Vegetables and fruits can also be cooked from frozen, but meats and fish should be thawed first. The only time food can be refrozen is when the food has been thawed thoroughly then cooked. Once the food has cooled, then it can be frozen again. On such occasions the food can only be stored for one month.

All poultry and game (except for duck) must be cooked thoroughly. When cooked, the juices will

run clear from the thickest part of the bird – the best area to try is usually the thigh. Other meats, like minced meat and pork should be cooked right the way through. Fish should turn opaque, be firm in texture and break easily into large flakes.

When cooking leftovers, make sure they are reheated until piping hot and that any sauce or soup reaches boiling point first.

STORING
REFRIGERATING AND FREEZING

M eat, poultry, fish, seafood and dairy products should all be refrigerated. The temperature of the refrigerator should be between 1–5°C/ 34–41°F while the freezer temperature should not rise above -18°C/-4°F.

To ensure the optimum refrigerator and freezer temperature, avoid leaving the door open for a long time. Try not to overstock the refrigerator as this reduces the airflow inside and affects the effectiveness in cooling the food within.

When refrigerating cooked food, leave it to cool down quickly and completely before refrigerating. Hot food will raise the temperature of the refrigerator and possibly affect or spoil other food stored in it.

Food within the refrigerator and freezer should always be covered. Raw and cooked food should be stored in separate parts of the refrigerator. Cooked food should be kept on the top shelves of the refrigerator, while raw meat, poultry and fish should be placed on bottom shelves to avoid drips and cross-contamination. It is recommended that eggs should be refrigerated in order to maintain their freshness and shelf life.

Take care that frozen foods are not stored in the freezer for too long. Blanched vegetables can be stored for one month; beef, lamb, poultry and pork for six months and unblanched vegetables and fruits in syrup for a year. Oily fish and sausages should be stored for three months. Dairy products can last four to six months while cakes and pastries should be kept in the freezer for three to six months.

HIGH-RISK FOODS

 ertain foods may carry risks to people who are considered vulnerable such as the elderly, the ill, pregnant women, babies, young infants and those suffering from a recurring illness.

It is advisable to avoid those foods listed below which belong to a higher-risk category.

There is a slight chance that some eggs carry the bacteria salmonella. Cook the eggs until both the yolk and the white are firm to eliminate this risk. Pay particular attention to dishes and products incorporating lightly cooked or raw eggs, which should be eliminated from the diet. Sauces including Hollandaise, mayonnaise, mousses, soufflés and meringues all use raw or lightly cooked eggs, as do custard-based dishes, ice creams and sorbets. These are all considered high-risk foods to the vulnerable groups mentioned above.

Certain meats and poultry also carry the potential risk of salmonella and so should be cooked thoroughly until the juices run clear and there is no pinkness left. Unpasteurised products such as milk, cheese (especially soft cheese), pâté, meat (both raw and cooked) all have the potential risk of listeria and should be avoided.

When buying seafood, buy from a reputable source, which has a high turnover to ensure freshness. Fish should have bright clear eyes, shiny skin and bright pink or red gills. The fish should feel stiff to the touch, with a slight smell of sea air and iodine. The flesh of fish steaks and fillets should be translucent with no signs of discoloration. Molluscs such as scallops, clams and mussels are sold fresh and are still alive. Avoid any that are open or do not close when tapped lightly. In the same way, univalves such as cockles or winkles should withdraw back into their shells when prodded lightly. When choosing cephalopods such as squid and octopus they should have a firm flesh and pleasant sea smell.

As with all fish, whether it is shellfish or seafish, care is required when freezing it. It is imperative to check whether the fish has been frozen before. If it has been frozen, then it should not be frozen again under any circumstances.

FRESH INGREDIENTS

T hai and Chinese cooking is amongst the world's greatest. In both, the basic philosophy of balance is the same, where the freshest produce is combined with the flavours of dried, salted and fermented ingredients, preserves and condiments. Most ingredients are now available in ordinary supermarkets and a few of the more unusual ones in Asian or Chinese groceries and markets.

AUBERGINES

Chinese aubergines are thinner with a more delicate flavour than the Mediterranean variety. They are used in many savoury dishes and in Thailand, some varieties are eaten raw with a dip or sauce.

BABY SWEETCORN

These tiny, tender cobs of sweetcorn, about 7.5 cm/ 3 inches long, add a crunchy texture and sweet flavour to many dishes. When buying, make sure that they are bright yellow with no brown patches, firm and crisp.

BAMBOO SHOOTS

Bamboo shoots are young, creamy-coloured, conical-shaped shoots of edible bamboo plants. They add a crunchy texture and clean, mild flavour

to many dishes and are sometimes available in Chinese groceries, as well as vacuum-packed or canned in most supermarkets. If you buy the latter, transfer them to a container of water once the can has been opened. If you change the water daily, they will keep for up to five days in the refrigerator.

BASIL

Holy basil with small, dark leaves and purple stalks is frequently used in Thai cooking, although sweet basil, more easily obtainable here, may be used instead.

BEANSPROUTS

These are the shoots of the mung bean and are readily available prepacked in the vegetable section of most supermarkets. They add a wonderfully crisp texture when added to stir-fries and take only a minute or two to cook. Ideally, the brown root should be removed from each sprout and discarded, however, this is time consuming, but improves the appearance of the dish.

BLACK BEANS

These small, black soya beans may also be known as salted black beans, as they have been fermented with salt and spices. Sold loose in Chinese groceries, but also available canned, they have a rich flavour and are often used with ginger and garlic with which they have a particular affinity.

BOK CHOI

Also known as pak choi, the most common variety has long, slightly ridged white stems like celery and large, oval thick dark green leaves. Bok choi has a mild, fresh, slightly peppery taste and needs very little cooking. Choose smaller ones if possible, as they are more tender. Store in the bottom of the refrigerator.

CHILLIES

There are many different kinds of chillies and generally, the smaller they

are the more fierce the heat. Red chillies are generally milder than green ones because they sweeten as they become riper. The tiny, slender tapering red or green Thai chillies are very hot and pungent. Thai cooks often include the seeds in cooking, but to moderate the heat, scrape out and discard the seeds.

CHINESE CELERY

Unlike the Western variety, Chinese celery stalks are thin, hollow and very crisp and range from pure white to dark green. Used as both a herb and a vegetable, Chinese celery is often stir-fried or used in soups and braised dishes.

CHINESE KALE

This green vegetable is popular in Thai cuisine. It has an almost earthy and slightly bitter taste and is usually served blanched and accompanied by oyster sauce. When buying, look for firm stems and fresh, dark green leaves. Store in the bottom drawer of the refrigerator for up to four days.

CHINESE KEYS

Despite its name, this root vegetable is often used in Thai cuisine and rarely in Chinese. It is a member of the ginger family, with an aromatic sweet flavour that goes well in Thai curries.

CHINESE LEAVES

Also known as Chinese cabbage, Chinese leaves look like a large, tightly packed lettuce with crinkly, pale green leaves. It adds a crunchy texture to stir-fries.

CHINESE MUSTARD CABBAGE

Also known as gaai choi, these mustard plants are similar in appearance to cabbages. The whole leaf is eaten, usually shredded into soups and stir-fries to which they add a fresh astringent flavour.

CORIANDER

Fresh coriander is the most popular fresh herb used in Thai cooking. It has an appearance similar to flat-leaf parsley, but has a pungent, slightly citrus flavour. Leaves, stems and roots are all used, so buy in big fresh bunches if possible.

DURIAN

This large, spiky-skinned tropical fruit has such an unpleasantly strong aroma that it is banned from public transport and hotels in Bangkok. It is expensive to buy a whole fruit, but you can sometimes buy frozen packs of skinless pieces of fruit.

GALANGAL

This is a rhizome, called *laos* or *ka* in Thailand. It is similar to ginger, but the skin is a pinkish colour

than you need it can be used within a week. Store it in the freezer as it can be grated from frozen.

KAFFIR LIME LEAVES

Dark green, smooth, glossy leaves, these come from the kaffir lime tree and are highly sought after for Thai cooking. They add a distinctive citrus flavour to curries, soups and sauces. Buy them from larger supermarkets and Oriental grocery shops and keep them in a sealed polythene bag in the freezer. Lime zest can be used as an alternative.

KRACHAI

Also known as lesser ginger, this is smaller and more spicy than either ginger or galangal. It can be bought fresh in Oriental food shops or dried in small packets.

LEMON GRASS

These look a bit like spring onions, but are much tougher. The stems should be bashed to release the lemony flavour during cooking, then removed before serving. Alternatively, peel away the outer layers and chop the heart very finely.

LOTUS ROOT

This is the underwater rhizome of the lotus flower and has a lacy appearance when sliced and a sweet, crunchy flavour. Fresh lotus root takes about two hours to cook, so it is worth considering using canned lotus root instead.

MANGETOUT

These tender green pea pods with flat, barely formed peas have a deliciously crisp texture. To prepare them for cooking, simply top and tail, pulling away any string from the edges.

MOOLI

Also known as daikon or white radish, these look like smooth, white parsnips (they come from the same family as the radish). They have a peppery, fresh taste and are often used in salads, peeled and thinly sliced or grated. They can also be cooked, but because they have a high water content, they should be salted to extract some of the liquid, then

and the flavour more complex and mellow. Peel it thinly and slice or grate the flesh. When sliced, it can be kept in an airtight container in the refrigerator for up to two weeks. If unavailable, ginger is an acceptable substitute.

GARLIC

This popular seasoning flavours almost all Thai and many Chinese dishes. In Thailand, garlic heads are smaller and thinner skinned, so they are often used whole as well as finely chopped or crushed. Choose firm garlic, preferably with a pinkish tinge and store in a cool, dry place, but not in the refrigerator.

GINGER

Fresh root ginger has a pungent, spicy, fresh taste. It is usually peeled, then finely chopped or grated – vary the amount of ginger used to suit your own taste. For just a hint, slice thickly and add to the dish when cooking, then remove just before serving. Fresh ginger is infinitely preferable to the powdered variety, which loses its flavour rapidly. Fresh ginger should feel firm when you buy it. If you have more rinsed well and steamed or boiled. They are often carved into beautiful and intricate shapes as a table decoration or garnish.

MUSHROOMS

Oyster mushrooms with their subtle flavour and delicate, almost slippery texture often feature in Chinese cooking. Now cultivated, they are widely available. The colour of the fan-shaped cap gives the mushroom its name, although they can also be pink or yellow as well as grey. Tear into long triangular segments, following the lines of the gills, and cook the smaller ones whole. Shiitake mushrooms were originally Oriental, but they are now grown all over the world. They are more often used dried in Chinese cooking, but may also be used fresh – the caps have a strong flavour and are generally sliced and the stalks discarded. Cook the mushrooms gently for a short time, as they may toughen if overcooked. Straw mushrooms are sometimes known as double mushrooms because that is exactly what they look like; two mushrooms that grow end to end. They are small and pale brown with a pale-coloured stem.

PAPAYA

Also called pawpaw, the unripe green flesh of this tropical fruit is often used in Thai cooking. It ripens to a deep orange colour and is delicious sliced and served as a dessert.

SHALLOTS

Small, mild-flavoured members of the onion family, shallots have coppery-coloured skins. Use them in the same way as onions, or thinly slice and deep-fry to use as a garnish.

SPRING ONIONS

Long, slender spring onions are the immature bulbs of yellow onions. They are frequently used in stir fries, as they cook within minutes.

TAMARIND

This adds an essential sour taste to many dishes. It is extracted from the pods as a sticky brown pulp, which is soaked to make tamarind water.

TOFU

Tofu or bean curd has been used as an ingredient in Thai and Chinese cooking for over 1000 years. Made from yellow soya beans, which are soaked, ground and briefly cooked, tofu is very rich in protein and low in calories. Because of its bland taste it is ideal cooked with stronger flavourings. It is usually available in two types: a soft variety known as silken tofu that can be used for soups and desserts, and a firm, solid white block, which can be cubed or sliced and included in stir-frying and braising. Also available is smoked tofu, which is a seasoned bean curd. When using, cut into the required size with care and do not stir too much when cooking; it simply needs to be heated through.

WATER CHESTNUTS

These are bulbs of an Asian water plant that look like and are a similar size to chestnuts. When peeled, the inner flesh is very crisp. Some Oriental grocers sell them fresh, although canned, either whole or sliced, are almost as good.

WATER SPINACH

This is widely grown throughout Asia and is unrelated to ordinary spinach. The leaves are elongated and tender and the stems fine and delicate. Water spinach requires minimal cooking. It is cooked in the same way as spinach, either steamed, stir-fried or added to soups.

YARD-LONG BEANS

Although unrelated to French beans, they are similar in appearance, but about four times longer. As they grow, they start to curl and are often sold in looped bunches. Two varieties exist: a pale green type and a much darker, thinner variety. They are very popular and may be found in great quantities in Chinese markets. The Cantonese often cook them with black beans or fermented bean curd and in Sichuan, they are deep-fried. Store in a plastic bag in the refrigerator for up to four days. To prepare, cut into lengths and use in exactly the same way as French beans.

DRY, CANNED AND PRESERVED INGREDIENTS

BIRD'S NEST

This is literally a bird's nest made from the spittle of a swallow and can occasionally be found in Chinese food shops. It is sold as a crunchy jelly that is often added to sauces, soups and extravagant stuffings and is an acquired taste. Since it is dried, it can be stored in a dry place for several years. To use, it should be soaked overnight in cold water, then simmered for 20 minutes in fresh water.

CASHEW NUTS

These milky-flavoured nuts with a crunchy texture, are often used whole or chopped in Chinese cooking, particularly as an ingredient in chicken dishes.

CASSIA

This is the bark taken from a cassia or laurel tree and is dark brown and flat in shape. It is similar, but slightly less subtle than cinnamon.

CHILLIES

Dried red chillies are used throughout Thailand and in many regions of China. The drying process concentrates the flavour, making them more fiery. Look for dried chillies with a bright red colour and a pungent aroma. If stored in a sealed container, they will keep almost indefinitely. Chilli oil is made from crushed dried chillies or whole fresh chillies and is used as both a seasoning and a dipping condiment. Chilli powder is made from dried red chillies and is usually mixed with other spices and seasonings, ranging from mild and aromatic to very hot – always check the jar before using. Chilli bean sauce is a thick, dark paste made from soya beans, chillies and other spicy seasonings and is very hot. Seal the jar after use and store in the refrigerator.

COCONUT MILK

Rich, creamy coconut milk is extracted from the white flesh of the nut. It can be bought in cans or made by adding boiling water to a sachet of coconut powder. Sometimes an opaque, white cream rises to the top of canned coconut milk and solidifies. You should shake the can before opening. If the milk is stored in an airtight container in the refrigerator it will last for up to three days, however, it does not freeze well. Occasionally, freshly made coconut milk may be bought from Oriental groceries. It is often used in Thai cooking, especially in curries and may also be used in desserts.

CORIANDER

Ground coriander is made from coriander seeds and has an almost sweet, spicy, fresh flavour. You can buy it ready ground or instead toast whole seeds in the oven and grind them yourself.

CREAMED COCONUT

Made from coconut oils and other fats, this comes in a hard, white block. It is not a substitute for coconut milk and is usually added at the end of cooking, to thicken a sauce, or to add coconut flavour to a finished dish.

GROUNDNUT OIL

Also known as peanut oil, this has a mild, nutty flavour. Because it can be heated to high temperatures, it is ideal for both stir-frying and deep-frying.

HOISIN SAUCE

This is a thick, dark brownish-red sauce, which is sweet, tangy and spicy. Made from soya beans, salt, flour, sugar, vinegar, chilli, garlic and sesame oil, it may be used as a dip, in 'red-cooking' and as a baste for roasted meats.

MUSHROOMS

Many sorts of dried mushrooms are used in Thai and Chinese cooking. Cloud ear (black fungus) mushrooms need soaking in warm water for about 20 minutes before use. They have a subtle, mild flavour and are highly regarded for their colour and gelatinous flavour. Dried shiitake mushrooms have a very strong flavour and are used in small quantities. After soaking, the hard stalks are usually discarded or added to stock.

NAM PLA FISH SAUCE

This is a golden brown, thin sauce with a salty flavour and is made from salted and fermented fresh fish, usually anchovies. It is used in Thai cooking in much the same way as soy sauce is used in Chinese cooking. The fishy aroma is almost unpleasant when the bottle is opened, but this mellows when mixed with other ingredients, adding a unique Thai flavour.

NOODLES

There are many types of noodles used in Thai and Chinese cuisine. The most popular include: cellophane noodles – also known as glass noodles – that are white and become transparent when cooked. Made from ground mung beans, they are never served on their own, but are added to soups or are deep-fried and used as a garnish. Egg noodles can be bought fresh, but the dried ones, which come in fine and medium, are just as good. Generally, flat noodles are used in soups and round ones for stir-fries. Rice noodles are fine, opaque noodles made from rice flour and are also called rice sticks. They are common in southern China, as it is the rice growing area of the country. Wheat is the primary grain in northern China and is made into noodles without egg. These noodles are sold in compressed square packages and bundles. *Yifu* noodles are round, yellow noodles, woven in a round cake and are often sold precooked.

OYSTER SAUCE

This is a thick, brown sauce made from oysters cooked in soy sauce. It has a wonderfully rich, but not fishy flavour, as this disappears during processing. Often used as a condiment, it is also one of the most used ingredients in southern Chinese cuisine.

PLUM SAUCE

As the name suggests, plum sauce is made from plums that are simmered together with vinegar, sugar, ginger, chilli and other spices.

RICE

Glutinous rice is a short-grain variety often used in desserts. It is sometimes referred to as sticky rice. Thai Jasmine rice is a long-grain rice from Thailand with an aromatic and subtle flavour.

RICE PAPER

This is made from a mixture of rice flour, water and salt, which is rolled out by machine until it is paper-thin and dried. It comes in round or triangular pieces which can be softened by placing between two damp tea towels and are then used to make spring rolls.

RICE VINEGARS

There are several varieties: white vinegar is clear and mild; red vinegar is slightly sweet and quite salty and is often used as a dipping sauce; black vinegar is very rich, yet mild and sweet vinegar is very thick, dark-coloured and flavoured with star anise.

RICE WINE

Often used in Chinese cooking in both marinades and sauces, rice wine is made from glutinous rice and has a rich, mellow taste. Do not confuse rice wine with sake, which is the Japanese version, as it is very different. Pale dry sherry is a good substitute for rice wine.

SESAME OIL

This is a thick, dark-golden to brown aromatic oil that is made from sesame seeds. It is rarely used in frying, as it has a low smoke-point, but when it is, it should be combined with another oil. It is often added to a finished dish in small quantities.

SESAME PASTE

Sesame paste is a rich, very creamy brown paste made from sesame seeds, however, it is not the same as tahini paste from the Middle-East. If unavailable, use smooth peanut butter, which has a similar texture.

SESAME SEEDS

These are the dried seeds of the sesame herb. Unhulled, the seeds may be dull white to black in colour, but once the hull is removed, the seeds are a creamy-white colour. Sesame seeds are often used as

a garnish or as a light coating to add crunch to food. Toast them first, to intensify their flavour, by shaking over heat in a dry frying pan until the seeds are lightly coloured.

SHRIMP PASTE

Made from puréed, fermented salted shrimps, this is popular in Thai cooking and adds a distinctive fishy flavour. There is also a Chinese version, which has an even stronger aroma. Use both sparingly. Dried salted shrimps are also available, which are sometimes used as a seasoning in stir-fries. They should be soaked first in warm water, then puréed in a blender or made into a paste with a pestle and mortar.

SOY SAUCE

Both light and dark soy sauce feature frequently in Chinese and Thai cooking. It is made from a mixture of soya beans, flour and water that are fermented together and allowed to age. The resulting liquid which is then distilled is soy sauce. Light soy sauce has a lighter colour and is more salty than the dark variety. It is often labelled as 'superior soy'. Dark soy sauce is aged for longer and the colour is almost black. Its flavour is stronger and is slightly thicker than light soy sauce. Confusingly, this is labelled in Thai and Chinese food shops as 'Soy Superior Sauce'. It is also possible to buy a mushroom soy sauce, which is made by the infusion of dry straw mushrooms and a shrimp-flavoured soy sauce.

STAR ANISE

This is an eight-pointed, star-shaped pod with a strong aniseed flavour. It is added whole to many Chinese dishes, but is usually removed before serving. It is also a vital ingredient in Chinese five spice powder.

SUGAR

Added in small quantities to many savoury Thai dishes, sugar balances the flavour of a dish, and gives a shiny appearance to the sauces. Thai palm sugar comes in large lumps or slabs, which need to be bashed with a mallet, to break into smaller pieces. Brown coffee crystals make a good alternative.

SZECHUAN PEPPERCORNS

This small reddish spice has a distinct, woody flavour and is more fragrantly spicy than hot. It is one of the spices in Chinese five spice powder. Also known as *fargara* and Chinese pepper, Szechuan peppercorns are used extensively in Sichuan cooking. Unrelated to peppers, they are the dried berries of a shrub and have a slight numbing effect on the tongue.

THAI CURRY PASTE

Red curry paste is a strongly flavoured spicy paste made mainly from dried red chillies that are blended with other spices and herbs. There is also green curry paste, which is hotter and made from fresh green chillies.

THOUSAND-YEAR-OLD EGGS

Fresh duck eggs are often preserved in brine, which seeps into the shell, making the whites salty and the yolks firm and orange-coloured. Thousand-year-old eggs are preserved in a mixture of clay, fine ash and salt. The whites of the eggs turn a translucent black and the yolks a grey-green colour after a year or so, hence their name. Unopened eggs can be kept for many months.

TURMERIC

This mild flavoured spice adds a bright yellow hue to foods. Although it can sometimes be bought fresh, it is most often used in its dried powdered form. Wonton wrappers, also called wonton skins, are egg and flour pastry-like wrappings that can be stuffed then fried, steamed or added to soups. Fresh ones may be stored for about five days in the refrigerator if kept wrapped in clingfilm.

YELLOW BEAN SAUCE

This thick, aromatic sauce is made with fermented yellow beans, flour and salt and adds a distinctive flavour to sauces.

EQUIPMENT AND TECHNIQUES

T here are numerous pieces of equipment that are very useful for stir-frying. Most can be bought very cheaply from Oriental grocers, or often more expensively from department stores.

EQUIPMENT
WOK

The most useful piece of equipment is, of course, the wok. It is much easier to use than a frying pan because of its depth, making it easier to toss the food around quickly without spilling it. A wok also requires a lot less oil for deep-frying than a deep-fat fryer, although more care is required in terms of safety. Another advantage is that the shape of the wok allows heat to spread more evenly, ensuring that the food cooks much more quickly.

There are a number of shapes of wok available. The Cantonese wok has short handles on each side. This type of wok is best for steaming and deep-frying because it is easier to move when full of liquid. The Pau wok has a single handle and is better for stir-frying, allowing you to manoeuvre the pan with one hand while stirring the food with the other one.

Woks can also have rounded or slightly flattened bases. Round-bottomed woks are really only suitable for use on gas hobs. Flattened-bottomed woks can be used on gas and electric hobs but are better for deep-frying than stir-frying.

When choosing a wok, look for a large one simply because it is easier to cook a small amount in a large wok than a large amount in a small one. Choose a wok that is heavy and made of carbon steel, rather than stainless steel or aluminium,

which tend to scorch. Non-stick woks are also available but these cannot be seasoned or used over very high temperatures, both of which are essential for flavour in stir-frying. Electric woks are also available, but these cannot be heated sufficiently hot enough and tend to have very shallow sides. They also lack the manoeuvrability of a free-standing wok.

If you buy a carbon-steel wok, it will need to be seasoned before use. First, scrub well using a cream cleanser or another abrasive to remove the machine oil with which it will probably have been coated to prevent rusting. Dry it well and then place it over a low heat. Add a little cooking oil and rub this all over the cooking surface with wadded kitchen paper. Continue heating over a low heat for 10–15 minutes, then wipe well with more kitchen paper – the paper will blacken. Repeat this process of coating, heating and wiping until the kitchen paper comes away clean. With continued use, the wok will darken further.

Do not scrub a seasoned wok with soap and water. Wash in hot, plain water using a brush or non-stick scrubber. Dry thoroughly with absorbent kitchen paper and place over a low heat until completely dry. Rub with a few drops of cooking oil to prevent rusting. If a little rust does appear, scrub off with cream cleanser or another abrasive and repeat the seasoning process.

ACCESSORIES

If your hob will not support a free-standing wok, Oriental stores sell metal rings or frames, called wok stands, that stabilize round-bottomed woks. These stands are an essential piece of equipment, so if you plan on doing a lot of steaming, deep-frying or braising in your wok it may be worth purchasing one. The stands are available in two designs: one is a solid ring punched with ventilation holes and the other is a circular wire frame. Only use the wire frame stand if you have a gas hob as the other stand will not allow sufficient ventilation.

You may also find it useful to have a lid for your wok. Wok lids are dome-like in shape, are usually made from aluminium and are very

inexpensive. Any large, dome-shaped pan lid that fits snugly over the wok will suffice. Alternatively, use kitchen foil.

A long-handled spatula is also an important piece of equipment. Special spatulas with rounded ends are readily available and make stirring and tossing food in the wok much easier. A long-handled spoon can be used instead.

If you are going to use the wok as a steamer, a wooden or metal rack or trivet is also a useful tool, as it holds the plate or steamer above the water.

Chinese cooks would not be without a cleaver. It differs from a meat cleaver in that a Chinese cleaver has a finer, much sharper blade and is used for all kinds of cutting, from shredding to chopping up bones. Several types of Chinese cleavers are available including a light-weight, narrow-bladed cleaver for cutting delicate foods such as vegetables, a medium-weight model for general use and a heavy cleaver for heavy-duty chopping.

For steaming, it may be worth investing in a bamboo steamer. They are both attractive and

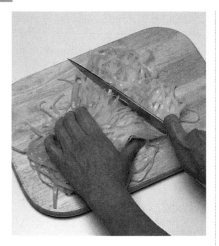

effective. They come in a variety of sizes and stack together with the uppermost basket having a lid. Fill the steamer with food, placing the food needing the longest cooking time in the bottom basket and the more delicate foods in the top basket. Stand the steamer on a trivet in a steady wok of boiling water. Cover tightly and leave to cook.

Another useful piece of equipment if you plan to do a lot of cooking in the wok is an electric rice cooker. It will cook rice perfectly and keep it warm, sometimes up to several hours. It also has the advantage of freeing-up cooker space. They are relatively expensive, however, but if you cook rice frequently it may be worth buying.

Chopsticks are used in Chinese and Japanese cookery not just for eating but for stirring, beating and whipping. They are available in wood and plastic and can be bought in Oriental grocers and department stores. Chinese chopsticks are larger with blunted ends, while Japanese chopsticks tend to be smaller with pointed ends.

To use chopsticks, put one chopstick into the crook of your preferred hand, between your thumb and first finger, holding the chopstick about two-thirds of the way up from the thinner

end. Let it rest on your third finger. Put the second chopstick between your thumb and fore-finger so that its tip is level with the chopstick below. Keep the lower chopstick steady and move the top one to pick up food.

TECHNIQUES

The initial preparation of food in wok cooking is probably more important than the cooking itself. Most dishes are cooked very rapidly, so it is im-portant that everything is prepared beforehand and is chopped into small, even-sized pieces to ensure quick, even cooking without overcooking. This type of preparation also ensures the dish looks attractive.

Wok cookery covers a number of different cooking methods – sometimes in one recipe – and most are easily mastered. When planning a meal, make sure you select dishes using different cooking methods and only one that is stir-fried.

CUTTING TECHNIQUES

SLICING Several different types of slicing methods are useful in wok and stir-fry cooking, including the conventional method of laying the food firmly on a chopping board and slicing straight down to cut the food into thin slices. Meat is always sliced across the grain to break up the fibres and to make it more tender when cooked. If you use a cleaver, hold the cleaver with your index finger over the far side of the top of the cleaver and your thumb on the side nearest to you and guide the cutting edge firmly through the food. With your other hand, hold the food and make sure when cutting that you turn your fingers under for safety.

CHOPPING This is the simplest technique and refers to simply cutting food through. With whole birds or cooked food with bones which needs to be chopped into smaller pieces, place on a firm surface, then using a straight, sharp, downward motion, chop through the bones, hitting down with the blade, then finish off the blow with the flat of your other hand on the top edge of the knife or cleaver. A heavy cleaver or knife is best for these tasks.

DIAGONAL SLICING This is particularly useful for vegetables as it exposes more surface area to the heat of the wok and also makes the food look much more interesting. Simply angle the knife or cleaver against the food and slice. For larger vegetables such as courgettes, carrots and aubergines, make one diagonal cut at the end of the vegetable. Turn the vegetable 90 degrees, cut in half lengthways, then diagonally slice each half. Continue until the whole vegetable has been chopped into even-sized pieces.

DICING This is a simple technique of cutting food into small cubes or dice. First cut the food into slices as for shredding. Stack the slices and slice again lengthways into sticks, again as you would for shredding. Turn the sticks again and cut crossways into cubes.

HORIZONTAL OR FLAT SLICING This is a technique for slicing whole foods thinly, while retaining the overall shape. A cleaver is particularly useful for this technique. Hold the knife or cleaver with the blade parallel to the chopping board. Place your free hand on top of the food to be sliced. Using a gentle slicing motion, slice sideways into the food and right the way through, taking care to keep your upper hand out of the way. This is particularly useful for splitting chicken breasts and similar meats.

MINCING This is a very fine chopping technique. First slice the food and then chop it rapidly – it will spread out over the chopping area. Gather it into a pile and continue chopping and regathering until the food is chopped as finely as needed. If very fine results are required, a food processor may be a better tool to use, but be careful not to overprocess.

SCORING This is used to score the surface of foods, such as duck breasts and squid to help them cook faster and evenly and to give them an attractive appearance. Use a cleaver or sharp knife and make shallow cuts into the food at a slight angle. Take care not to cut all the way through. Make cuts right across the food, then turn and make a second series of cuts at an angle to the first set to make diamond shapes.

SHREDDING This is cutting food into fine, matchstick shreds. First cut the food into slices, then stack the slices and cut again, lengthways this time, into fine shreds. It is sometimes easier to cut meat and fish if they have been placed in the freezer for 20–30 minutes before slicing.

OTHER USEFUL TECHNIQUES

Marinating This is a common process in Chinese and other Oriental cookery to add flavour to meat, fish and vegetables. The food is steeped in a mixture of flavours, which could include soy sauce, rice wine, garlic, ginger or spices. Marinating time is usually at least 20 minutes, but often can be as long as overnight. Food is usually removed from the marinade before cooking.

THICKENING There are two useful ways of thickening sauces. The first is to use cornflour mixed until smooth with a little water that is then whisked into the hot, not boiling, sauce. The sauce is brought up to the simmer and cooked gently for about 2 minutes until thickened. The other method of thickening is to reduce the sauce; the liquid is simmered until most of the excess liquid has boiled off, leaving a concentrated and thickened sauce.

VELVETING This is a particularly useful technique in Chinese cooking which helps to protect delicate foods, such as chicken breasts, from overcooking. The food is coated with a mixture of cornflour and egg white and sometimes salt. The mixture is marinated in the refrigerator for 20–30 minutes before cooking.

COOKING TECHNIQUES

BLANCHING This method involves cooking food in boiling water or moderately hot oil for a few minutes so that it is partly cooked, which speeds up the cooking process later on, so that other elements of the dish do not overcook. Chicken is often blanched in oil after velveting, meat is often blanched in water to remove excess fat and vegetables are often blanched in water, drained and refreshed under cold water, before being drained again and dried. In the case of vegetables, stir-frying merely heats them through and finishes the cooking.

BRAISING This is a method often applied to tougher cuts of meat that need long, slow cooking times to remain moist. The food is usually browned and then cooked in stock or liquid to

which other flavourings are also added. The mixture is brought up to simmering point and then cooked gently until tender.

DEEP-FRYING This is another very important technique in Far Eastern cookery. Woks are very useful for deep-frying as they use far less oil than conventional deep-fat fryers. Although a deep-fat fryer is safer, a few precautions mean that deep-frying in a wok is very easy. Ensure that the wok sits securely on the hob, either by using a flat-bottomed wok or a wok stand. Carefully add the oil, ensuring that the wok is no more than half full. Heat up slowly to the required temperature.

To test for temperature, either use a thermometer made for the purpose or the following test. Add a small cube of crustless bread and time how long it takes to brown. Generally, if the bread browns in 30 seconds, the oil is at the correct temperature. If it browns more quickly the oil is too hot. If it takes longer to brown the oil is too cold. Allow the oil to return to the correct temperature between batches of food and do not overfill the wok. Do not leave the wok unsupervised on the stove when deep frying.

It is also important that food to be deep-fried is dry. Lift food from a marinade and blot thoroughly on kitchen paper. If using batter, allow any excess to drip off before adding to the oil.

Oil used for deep-frying can be reused. Allow the oil to cool completely and then strain into a clean jar or other container. Label the jar with the type of food the oil was used for and only reuse it for the same type of food. Oil can be reused up to 3 times.

POACHING This is a method of cooking meat or fish in simmering liquid until nearly cooked so that it can be added to soup or combined with a sauce to finish the cooking.

SHALLOW-FRYING This is similar to sautéing as it involves more oil than stir-frying, but less than deep-frying. Food is fried first on one side and then on the other. Often the excess oil is drained off and a sauce is made in the same pan. A frying pan is preferable for shallow-frying rather than a wok.

SLOW-SIMMERING AND STEEPING Slow-simmered food is cooked very gently in liquid that just simmers. Simmering is the method for making stock. Steeping is a similar method, except that the heat is turned off and the heat of the liquid alone finishes off the cooking process.

STEAMING Steaming is an ancient technique currently enjoying a revival because it adds no fat to the food being cooked. Steamed foods are cooked on a gentle, moist heat. Steaming is particularly suited to vegetable and fish.

Woks can be used as steamers in two ways. The first method is described under the section on bamboo steamers. The second method involves putting about 5 cm/2 inches of water in a stable wok on the hob. A metal or wooden rack or trivet is then placed into the wok and the water is brought to the boil. The food to be steamed should be arranged on a plate and the plate should be lowered on to the rack. The wok then needs to be covered tightly with a lid. For longer cooking times, the water may need replenishing.

STIR-FRYING This is the most famous of wok cooking techniques and is used throughout China and the Far East as well as in India. It is possibly the most tricky of wok techniques because it involves a lot of preparation as well as a good source of heat. Its advantage is that stir-fried foods can be cooked very quickly in very little oil so that they retain their colour, flavour and texture. It is very important that stir-fried foods are not greasy or overcooked.

TWICE-COOKING As the name implies, this is a two-step process involving two different techniques, such as simmering and stir-frying. For example, pork ribs may be gently simmered to remove the excess fat before draining and stir-frying or braising with other flavours.

STEPS TO STIR-FRYING
(ONCE ALL THE INGREDIENTS ARE PREPARED AND TO HAND):

* Heat the wok or frying pan over the highest heat until it is very hot before adding the oil. This prevents the food from sticking and en-sures an even heat. Add the oil and using a spatula or long-handled spoon, distribute it evenly over the surface. It should be very hot – almost smoking – before you add any ingredients (unless you are adding flavouring ingredients). If you are flavour-ing the oil, for example with garlic, ginger, spring onions or chilli (or a combination) do not let the oil become smoking hot because these types of ingredients will burn at such high temperatures and become bitter. Add to hot but not smoking oil and toss the ingredients around quickly for a few seconds. In some recipes these ingredients are removed and discarded.

* Now add the next ingredients as described in the recipe and proceed to stir-fry by tossing quickly in the wok using a spatula or long-handled spoon. When cooking meat, allow it to rest for a few seconds between stirring. Otherwise keep the food moving, transferring it from the bottom to the sides of the wok and back again. Because of the high heat involved when stir-frying, there may be some spluttering and splattering of hot fat, so take care during this stage of cooking.

* Once everything is cooked, some stir-fried dishes are thickened with a mixture of cornflour and water. To avoid a lumpy sauce, make sure the mixture is smooth and reduce the heat to just below simmering point before adding it. Stir in the cornflour mixture then increase the heat to a simmer and cook for a further 2–3 minutes, until the sauce is thickened, smooth and coats all the ingredients.

GARNISHES

Oriental cuisines pay a lot of attention to the finished appearance of food and this is one reason for cutting ingredients carefully. Often dishes will be garnished attractively with anything from simple shredded chillies to more elaborate spring onion tassels. Thai cooks often go to elaborate lengths, carving flowers from carrots or making tomato roses as garnishes. In fact, the Thai Royal family employs an official Fruit Carver (a hereditary post) for special occasions. The home cook can create some simple effects with everyday ingredients and a sharp knife.

CHILLI FLOWERS Take a well-formed red chilli, about 5–7.5 cm/2–3 inches long, with the stem intact. Hold the chilli by the stem and, using a fine sharp knife, cut from the tip to the stem, at equal distances all the way around, without cutting through the stem. Try to leave the seeds intact. Gently pull back the strips and drop into iced water. The strips will curl back into a flower.

SPRING ONION tassels Trim the top green end of a spring onion and cut a piece about 5–7.5 cm/2–3 inches long, including about 1 cm/½ inch of the white base. With a fine, sharp knife, and holding the white part as a base, shred the green part as finely as possible. Drop into a bowl of iced water until the shreds curl back.

CLEAR CHICKEN & MUSHROOM SOUP

INGREDIENTS

Serves 4

2 large chicken legs, about 450 g/1 lb total weight
1 tbsp groundnut oil
1 tsp sesame oil
1 onion, peeled and very thinly sliced
2.5 cm/1 inch piece root ginger, peeled and very finely chopped
1.1 litres/2 pints clear chicken stock

1 lemon grass stalk, bruised
50 g/2 oz long-grain rice
75 g/3 oz button mushrooms, wiped and finely sliced
4 spring onions, trimmed, cut into 5 cm/2 inch pieces and shredded
1 tbsp dark soy sauce
4 tbsp dry sherry
salt and freshly ground black pepper

1 Skin the chicken legs and remove any fat. Cut each in half to make 2 thigh and 2 drumstick portions and reserve. Heat the groundnut and sesame oils in a large saucepan. Add the sliced onion and cook gently for 10 minutes, or until soft but not beginning to colour.

2 Add the chopped ginger to the saucepan and cook for about 30 seconds, stirring all the time to prevent it sticking, then pour in the stock. Add the chicken pieces and the lemon grass, cover and simmer gently for 15 minutes. Stir in the rice and cook for a further 15 minutes or until the chicken is cooked.

3 Remove the chicken from the saucepan and leave until cool enough to handle. Finely

shred the flesh, then return to the saucepan with the mushrooms, spring onions, soy sauce and sherry. Simmer for 5 minutes, or until the rice and mushrooms are tender. Remove the lemon grass.

4 Season the soup to taste with salt and pepper. Ladle into warmed serving bowls, making sure each has an equal amount of shredded chicken and vegetables and serve immediately.

FOOD FACT

Tahini is a thick paste made from sesame seeds. It is available from many delicatessens and supermarkets as well as Oriental food stores. It is most often used in making hummus.